HELLO!

HELLO KITTY

Annual 2012

© 1976, 2011 SANRIO CO., LTD.
978-0-00-742691-1
1
First published in the UK by
HarperCollins Children's Books in 2011
A CIP catalogue record for this title is available from
the British Library.
www.harpercollins.co.uk

Printed and bound in China.

HarperCollins *Children's Books*

Welcome to my 2012 Annual!
It's packed full of fun – there are games to play,
activities to do and things to make. Plus, you'll find lots
about my plans for 2012, which I'm sure will give you some ideas
of your own. I had a fantastic year last year, but something tells
me this year is going to be even better. So read on for all things
Hello Kitty, and have fun!

Love,

*Hello
Kitty
×× *

Contents

Hello, Hello Kitty!

Hello, I'm Hello Kitty!
This page will tell you everything
you need to know about me!

Name:
Hello Kitty

Birthday:
1st November

Star sign:
Scorpio

Height:
as tall as five apples

Weight:
as heavy as three apples

Lives:
in London with
my family.

**Favourite
colours:**
red, pink, blue.

Family:
Mary White
(mother), George White
(father), Mimmy (twin sister)

Friends:
Fifi, Dear Daniel,
Thomas, Jodie, Tippy,
Tracy, Tim and Tammy,
Joey, Moley, Rory.

Me in my garden.

My family at
the beach.

Check out my band!

On my way to photography club.

Mimmy and me, picking apples.

I love my tiara and sparkly jewellery!

My school.

Fifi, Thomas and Tracy.

Interests:
spending time with my friends, baking, travelling with my family, crafts, trying new things, fashion, photography.

Jodie, Tim and Tammy.

Me in a yellow cab in New York!

All about you

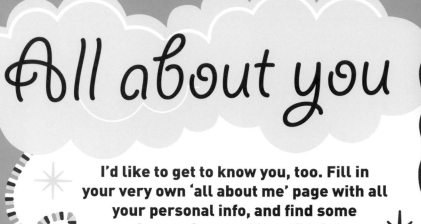

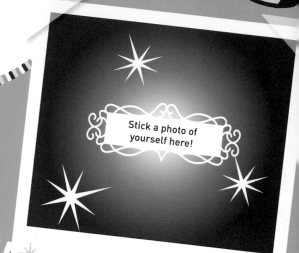

I'd like to get to know you, too. Fill in your very own 'all about me' page with all your personal info, and find some photos of yourself to stick in!

Stick a photo of yourself here!

Name: ....

Lives: ....

....

Birthday:
....

Star sign:
....

Favourite colours:
....
....

Family:
....
....
....

Interests (what do you enjoy doing?)
....
....
....
....

Friends:
....
....
....

Stick a photo of yourself here!

My friends

My family

Stick a photo of yourself here!

New year's resolutions

New year's resolutions are promises you make to yourself at the start of a new year. Take a look at mine – they might give you some ideas of your own!

This year, I will...

★ be friendly to new people.
★ try a new activity.
★ keep my room clean and tidy.
★ do something kind every day.
★ ask Mama and Papa for my own flowerbed.
★ eat five portions of fruit and vegetables a day.
★ enter a tennis tournament.
★ start my own fashion label!

Sometimes it can be tricky to keep new year's resolutions, but if you write them down and stick them somewhere obvious you will always have them in your mind. I know you can do it!

So what are your new year's resolutions? Write them in below, then at the end of the year, give yourself a mark out of five for how well you managed to keep them. Colour in the number of stars you think you deserve for each one!

This year, I will...

1. ....
2. ....
3. ....
4. ....
5. ....
6. ....
7. ....
8. ....
9. ....
10. ....

Stage style

Tonight is my band's first show, and I'm looking for the perfect outfit to wear. It's really important that I look super stylish. Can you help me find the right outfit, based on the list below? Circle the outfit you think is right for me.

★ Nothing blue
★ Nothing stripey
★ Nothing with hearts on
★ Nothing yellow
★ Nothing with spots on
★ Must have some red
★ Must be a skirt and top or a dress – no trousers

13

My notebook

I carry my notebook everywhere I go. I write all sorts of things inside: ideas for outfits, to-do lists, places I want to visit and fun things I have done that day. I also stick things in, like cinema tickets and photos. Here's a sneak peek into my entries from this week!

Monday

To-do:
★ Remember to make birthday card for Fifi! Use new glitter pens.
★ Tidy my bedroom.
★ Finish all my homework.
★ Playing tennis with Mimmy, 5pm

I like this dress!

Tuesday

★ Family trip to the bowling alley!
★ Make a collage for Mimmy's bedroom wall to say thank you for lending me her blue dress.
★ Find something to wear to the concert tonight.

Thomas

Wednesday

★ I've been invited to a sleepover at Tracy's house. Can't wait! Will ask Mama to help me bake some tasty midnight snacks.
★ Meet Fifi at the library, 1pm.
★ Remember to sponsor Thomas for his run.
★ Help Mama and Papa organize family barbecue. Find some yummy smoothie recipes.

Thursday

To-do:
- ✶ Make friendship bracelets for Fifi, Mimmy, Jodie, Tracy and Tammy.
- ✶ Make a fairy costume for Saturday.
- ✶ Make a get well soon card for Tippy.
- ✶ Write to Grandma and Grandpa.

My fairy costume!

Friday

Sleepover day! Mama taking me out in the morning to get:
- ✶ Ingredients for cookies
- ✶ New pyjamas
- ✶ A present for Tracy

Things to pack:
- ✶ Sleeping bag
- ✶ Pillow
- ✶ Pyjamas
- ✶ Toothbrush
- ✶ Face wash
- ✶ Clothes for Saturday
- ✶ Snacks!

Picture of my cookies!

Jodie and Fifi

Pretty princess

Being a princess looks like fun! Not many girls are lucky enough to be born into royalty, but there are lots of ways to make yourself look, and feel, like a princess.

♥ Act the part ♥

Be kind to everybody. Take time to talk to shy people or new people, as well as your friends.

Always be polite – princesses have perfect manners.

♥ Look the part ♥

Put on your favourite party dress and shoes, and accessorize with sparkly jewellery.

If you have a tiara, wear it!

Work hard, but make time to have fun, too. A princess knows how to do both!

Take care of your appearance. Princesses always look clean and tidy.

Princess bedroom ♥

Here are some ideas to get your bedroom looking regal:

Make some paper flowers for your desk or dressing table so you always have a beautiful bouquet in your room. You just need pipe cleaners, tissue paper and a vase. Cut your tissue paper into circles, push the pipe cleaner through the middle of your stack of circles, then scrunch up the tissue paper to look like petals. Pop them in a vase and they'll instantly brighten up your room!

Whatever you do, do it with style!

Make a princess door sign for your room. It could say 'The Princess Sleeps Here' or 'The Princess's Room'. Make it as pink as possible, and have a picture of yourself wearing a tiara or crown. You could use a photo and make a collage, or draw a picture of yourself.

Princesses love pretty ribbons! Tie back your curtains with ribbons and add them to your drawer handles or your headboard.

Green goddess

**I think being green is really cool, and lots of fun, too!
Here are my top tips on how to be a green goddess.**

Outdoors

Mama and Papa have given me my very own flowerbed, so I
can plant whatever plants I like and watch as they sprout up!
If you don't have a garden you can plant up window boxes.

These plants are very easy to
grow, and pretty, too:

pansies
sunflowers
wild strawberries
sweet peas
marigolds
nasturtiums

You will need:
★ a plant pot,
window box or a
flowerbed outside
★ soil or compost
★ a trowel
★ seeds
★ a watering can

1. Ask an adult to buy some seeds
for your chosen plant, then plant
them in your garden, in pots
or in window boxes (read the
instructions on the seed packet to
see which is best and how deep
to plant the seeds).

2. You can decorate plant pots and
window boxes with acrylic paint
to make them look pretty.

3. Make sure you water them regularly,
especially when you first plant them,
then watch as they sprout up!

We've also set up a water butt
to collect rainwater. Now we use
this to water the plants, instead
of a hosepipe.

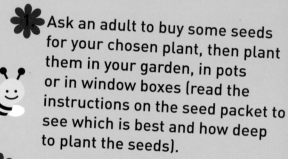

16

Indoors

Whenever you leave a room, remember to switch off the light to save energy. I asked Mama and Papa if we could use energy saving light bulbs in our house, too. Always turn off anything you aren't using, like the TV, stereo or games console, as well.

It's easy to leave the tap running when we're brushing our teeth, but if everybody turned the tap off we'd save a lot of water! Remember to switch it off next time, until you need to rinse your mouth.

Re-use and recycle
In my house, we always recycle things like paper, card, aluminium and plastic, but now I also use them to make collages, models or to decorate and store things in. You can do the same – take a look at this list of household items, and think of one thing you could make from each, then get crafting!

Cereal boxes..................................

Plastic bags..................................

Old clothes..................................

Shoe boxes..................................

Foil..................................

Egg boxes..................................

Plastic bottles..................................

Bottle tops..................................

Magazines..................................

Newspapers..................................

Old wrapping paper..................................

Old greetings cards..................................

Drinking straws..................................

Oops, something's gone wrong with my second set of photo prints!

20

HELLO KITTY

Travel time

I love travelling with my family and visiting new places. Here I am on some of my favourite trips.

Can you match the pictures to the places? Look at my outfits and the background detail to give you some clues.

a

b

HELLO KITTY SAFARI TOURS

c

d

1. Honolulu, Hawaii ......

2. New York, USA ......

3. Tokyo, Japan ......

4. Kenya, Africa ......

5. New Delhi, India ......

6. Paris, France ......

7. Dublin, Ireland ......

Super sleepovers

Make sure you get permission from an adult before planning a sleepover.

Talking with friends, pampering yourselves, snacking on delicious treats and snuggling up to watch a movie... sleepovers are so much fun! Here are my top tips for hosting the very best sleepovers in town.

Invitations

Why not make your own invitations for your sleepover? You could decorate them with pictures of sleeping bags, torches, pyjamas and snacks, or cut them into the shape of a sleeping bag or a pillow. You could also cut out the faces of your friends from photos and add them to the invitations. Why not have them poking out of sleeping bags? Send your invitations out a few weeks before your sleepover to give your guests plenty of time to reply.

Theme

Pick a theme for your sleepover. You could have a pink sleepover where everything is pink from the food to your pyjamas, a princess sleepover where everybody dresses up as a princess and you decorate your room to look like a palace, or a popstar sleepover where you dress as your favourite star and play singing games. Ask everybody to bring something that fits with the theme, and pick activities that fit, too.

Decorations

Choose a room to host your sleepover in. The living room or your bedroom would be perfect. Decorate your sleepover space so that you and your friends will feel like princesses! Blow up balloons, ask an adult to help you prepare some yummy snacks, then lay them out on the table or floor. Make sure there are plenty of soft cushions and blankets or chairs to sit on.

Activities

Pick some great girly DVDs or TV shows to watch. For very special sleepovers, e.g. for a special birthday, you could ask an adult to buy everybody a plain white pillowcase and have fun decorating them at your sleepover. Write your name, draw some doodles or ask your friends to sign yours using colourful pens. They'll be a great reminder of how much fun you had!

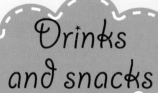

Drinks and snacks

I like to have lots of yummy snacks at my sleepovers. These delicious treats always go down well:

★ popcorn
★ nachos
★ pizza
★ grapes

★ strawberries
★ raspberries
★ lemonade
★ hot chocolate
★ fruit juice

Make sure everybody has somewhere to sleep (ask them to bring sleeping bags, pillows and duvets if you don't have enough), plenty of drinks and snacks, and let the fun begin!

Simple Sudoku

Sudoku puzzles are super fun! They are clever Japanese puzzles that teach your brain to be more logical. Usually they are made using numbers, but I've created some special ones of my own using pretty pictures. Can you finish them off by drawing in the missing symbols?

Rules

Each row down and across must contain only one of each symbol.

Now that you've got the hang of it, why not try some traditional number Sudoku puzzles? The rules are exactly the same – each row down and across must contain the numbers 1-4 only once.

Puzzle 1

		1	2
1	2		
		4	3
3	4		

Puzzle 2

		3	4
		2	1
1	2		
4	3		

Puzzle 3

3	1		
4	2		
		2	4
		3	1

Photo scrapbook

I've been having lots of fun sticking photos into my new photo scrapbook, but I need help writing captions for each photo. Can you help? Write a description of what we're doing under each picture.

....
....

Here we are camping in the forest. We toasted marshmallows and drank hot chocolate to keep warm!

....
....

....
....

....

....

....

....

....

....

....

....

....

....

What kind of friend are you?

My friends are really important to me. They each have different qualities that make them fantastic friends. Find out what kind of friend you are with this fun quiz! Circle your answer for each question, then add up how many as, bs and cs you get in total.

1 Your friends know they can rely on you...
a) to be there no matter what
b) to have lots of fun ideas
c) to give helpful advice

2 What do you like to talk about with your friends?
a) Good times – you love looking at old photos
b) The party next weekend
c) Their problems

3 You forgot your friend's birthday. What do you do?
a) I never forget a birthday!
b) Apologize, then plan a big surprise party
c) Apologize and ask what you can do to make it up to them

4 Two of your friends have fallen out. What do you do?
a) Side with your best friend, of course
b) Give them space to sort it out, then be ready with some fun activity ideas when they've made up
c) Help them work it out right away so you can all be friends again

5 What's your favourite thing to do with friends?
a) Sleepover so you can chat
b) Going to parties, playing games or having fun days out
c) Whatever they want to do

6 Your friend is sick. What do you do?
a) Go straight round with a present to cheer her up
b) Tell her lots of jokes and funny stories to make her laugh
c) Take her some yummy snacks and magazines and lend her your DVD collection to keep her entertained while she's sick

Results

Mostly as:

You are a loyal friend
Your friends are lucky to have you because you will always be on their side, no matter what. You have one or two best friends who you would do anything for.

Mostly bs:

You are a fun friend
You have lots of friends and love having fun. Your friends love you because you know how to make them giggle and keep life interesting.

Mostly cs:

You are a helpful friend
You are the problem solver of your group. You are thoughtful and caring and keen to help your friends out of sticky situations.

What's in my handbag?

I take my handbag with me everywhere I go. It's full of all the things I might need while I'm out and about.

Can you work out what's inside from this scan that was taken at the airport? Match the numbered shadows to the list of items on the right.

7

8

9

10

11

a. **Mobile phone** . . . .

b. **Umbrella** . . . .

c. **Apple** . . . .

d. **Perfume** . . . .

e. **Spare bow** . . . .

f. **Keys** . . . .

g. **Purse** . . . .

h. **Notebook** . . . .

i. **MP3 player and earphones** . . . .

j. **Comb** . . . .

k. **Sunglasses** . . . .

Messy Hello Kitty

I've been too busy to tidy my bedroom this week, and I can't find any of my bows. Can you help? I have 21 bows, including the one I'm wearing, so the other 20 could be anywhere!

Star signs

Your star sign can reveal a lot about you. There are twelve star signs in total, and you can find yours by checking below. Read about your friends' and family's star signs, too.

Aquarius

20th January – 18th February
Element: Air
Ruling planet: Uranus
Personality: Aquarius has lots of friends, and is known for being cheerful.

Taurus

20th April – 20th May
Element: Earth
Ruling planet: Venus
Personality: Taurus is a loyal friend and never gives up.

Pisces

19th February – 20th March
Element: Water
Ruling planet: Neptune
Personality: Pisces is creative and likes to dream.

Aries

21st March – 19th April
Element: Fire
Ruling planet: Mars
Personality: Aries is full of energy and ready for adventure!

Gemini

21st May – 20th June
Element: Air
Ruling planet: Mercury
Personality: Gemini is active and lively, and likes to chat to everyone!

Cancer

21st June – 22nd July
Element: Water
Ruling planet: the moon
Personality: Cancer is affectionate and great for a hug if you're having a bad day.

Leo

23rd July – 22nd August
Element: Fire
Ruling planet: the Sun
Personality: Leo is strong and brave and has lots of friends.

Sagittarius

22nd November – 21st December
Element: Fire
Ruling planet: Jupiter
Personality: Sagittarius is warm and loving, and ready for adventure.

Virgo

23rd August – 22nd September
Element: Earth
Ruling planet: Mercury
Personality: Virgo likes things to be perfect, and loves to learn about new things.

Capricorn

22nd December – 19th January
Element: Earth
Ruling planet: Saturn
Personality: Capricorn is sensible and has a great sense of humour.

Libra

23rd September – 22nd October
Element: Air
Ruling planet: Venus
Personality: Libra is friendly, open and generous.

Scorpio

23rd October – 21st November
Element: Water
Ruling planet: Pluto
Personality: Scorpio is clever and thinks a lot.

What does your element say about you?

Your element is also said to reveal things about your general personality.

★ **Earth** (Taurus, Virgo, Capricorn) Earth signs are practical and cautious and like to be organised.

★ **Air** (Gemini, Libra, Aquarius) Air signs are clever, curious and like to express themselves.

★ **Fire** (Aries, Leo, Sagittarius) Fire signs are active, enthusiastic, outgoing and confident.

★ **Water** (Cancer, Scorpio, Pisces) Water signs are sensitive, caring and artistic.

Apple maze

Mimmy and I have been apple picking in the forest, and now we're trying to get home. Can you help us ride back to our house, avoiding the fallen apples?

40

What's your favourite style?

Like any girl, I love experimenting with different styles. Find out what your favourite style is with this fun quiz!

1 Your favourite colour is
a) Pink
b) Black
c) White
d) Blue

2 What would you wear to your birthday party?
a) A sparkly dress
b) Jeans and a top
c) A pretty dress and matching leggings
d) A T shirt and tracksuit bottoms

3 What's in your bag?
a) Lip balm and a hairbrush
b) Your MP3 player
c) Your hairspray and mirror
d) Your gym kit

4 What does your bedroom look like?
a) Lots and lots of pink!
b) Covered in posters of your favourite band
c) Neat and tidy
d) Full of sports equipment

5 What's your favourite accessory?
a) Your tiara
b) Your sunglasses
c) Your posh jacket
d) Your baseball cap

6 **Your favourite shoes are...**
   a) Party shoes
   b) Black boots
   c) Smart black shoes
   d) Trainers

7 **How do you like to spend your weekend?**
   a) Dressing up
   b) Chilling out and listening to music
   c) Tidying your bedroom and planning your outfits for next week
   d) Playing sport

Results

Mostly as: Princess
You love all things pink and girly, and like to dress up to make yourself feel like a princess.

Mostly bs: Cool
You like to chill out and listen to music. Your style is cool and funky.

Mostly cs: Smart
You like to look your best at all times. You plan your outfits in advance and have a smart, colour-coordinated wardrobe.

Mostly ds: Sporty
You love being active and playing sport, and look super stylish in casual sports gear.

On your toes

Being active keeps you healthy and energized. This year I have lots of ideas for fun games to keep me on my toes. Why not try them out yourself? You don't need any special equipment, and you can play with friends or by yourself.

Obstacle course

Create a fun obstacle course for yourself and your friends, either inside or outside. You can time yourself if you have a clock or stopwatch, and compete with your friends to see who has the fastest lap time. If you're feeling particularly creative, you can make a rosette or a certificate for the winner.

★ Try to get a ball into a wastepaper basket (make sure it's light, so it won't break anything, and use balled-up paper if you prefer).

★ Set up objects in a zigzag pattern and weave in and out of them.

★ Ask an adult if you can have a sheet to lie on the floor and tunnel under.

★ Give yourself two sheets of newspaper and make your way from one side of the room to the other, using only those pieces of newspaper to step on (you will need to keep moving the paper).

Dance routine

Making up a dance routine, or 'choreography', is so much fun! Pick a track you'd like to dance to, then use your imagination to create a routine. Try watching some music videos for inspiration. Start moving to the music and see what you come up with! The tricky part is learning it by heart. Try writing down instructions for each move in your routine. Then you can perform your routine for your friends, and even teach it to them!
Remember to stretch before and after your dance routine.

Scavenger hunt

Make a list of things to find outdoors, and tick each one off when you see it, e.g. a pebble, a flower, a bird, an insect, tree bark, something that begins with the first letter of your name, something loud. You will need to take something to rest your paper on, like a clipboard, and a pen or pencil to tick things off.

Bike ride

Go for a bike ride with your friends or family. If the weather's nice, cycle to the park and have a picnic before cycling home again. Younger Hello Kitty fans should ask an adult before going out on a bike. And always wear a cycling helmet – it's the coolest headgear for bike riding!

Race to the Park

My friends and I are late for football practice. Can you help us dash through the town to get to the park? The first person there wins!

Players: Up to six players - you can be Hello Kitty, Mimmy, Fifi, Jodie, Thomas or Dear Daniel. You can use a different colour counter for each person. If you're feeling especially creative, make yourself some special counters by drawing a picture of each person on a circle of card.

You will need a counter for each player, and a die.

How to play: Take it in turns to roll the die and move the number of squares shown. Obey any instructions on the squares you land on.

Start here

Move forward a space

Move back two spaces

Miss a turn

Move forward a space

BAKERY

Miss a turn

Take another turn

Birthday cheer

Birthdays are very special, and should be celebrated in style! I love celebrating my birthday with family and friends, and making a fuss on their birthdays, too.

Do you know how to wish someone a happy birthday in a different language? Here are a few examples to start you off:

Italian:
Buon compleanno!

German:
Alles Gute zum Geburtstag!

French:
Joyeux anniversaire!

Chinese:
Sun Yat Fai Lok!

Indian (Hindi):
Janam Din ki badhai! or Janam Din ki shubkamnaayein!

Japanese:
Otanjoubi Omedetou Gozaimasu!

Spanish:
Feliz Cumpleaños!

Birthstones

A birthstone is a precious gemstone that symbolizes the month in which you were born.

Birthstones are expensive and very special presents, so if you have one, you are very lucky! Some people believe that surrounding yourself with the colour of your birthstone brings you good luck. Why not design a card or wrapping paper based on the colour of your friend's birthstone?

You could also make your friend a bouquet of paper flowers based on the colour of their birthstone (see page 17 for instructions).

I like to make birthday bracelets for my friends, using coloured string and beads to represent their birth month. It's very easy – all you have to do is tie a knot in one end of your string, thread your beads on, then tie both ends together. Mimmy made me a bracelet of orange beads for my birthday last year, and I love it! She even found two beads with my initials on them – H and K. It makes me feel lucky because orange is the colour of citrine, my birthstone!

You can buy beads from craft shops or on the internet. Birthday bracelets are the perfect birthday present for friends – they're personal and creative, and your friend will be touched that you put so much thought into their present.

Do you know what your birthstone is? Check the list below to find yours, then find your friends' birthstones, too!

 January: Garnet (dark red)

 February: Amethyst (purple)

 March: Aquamarine (light blue)

 April: Diamond (white)

 May: Emerald (green)

 June: Pearl or Moonstone (cream)

 July: Ruby (red)

 August: Peridot (light green)

 September: Sapphire (dark blue)

 October: Opal or Pink Tourmaline (white or pink)

 November: Topaz or Citrine (orange-yellow)

 December: Turquoise or Blue Topaz (sky blue)

Chocolate treats

Always ask an adult to help you in the kitchen.

Next time you need a special treat for a party or a gift, try one of my favourite chocolatey recipes. Mmm, delicious!

Truffles

Truffles are one of my favourite treats, and they're easy to make! Impress your friends at sleepovers or birthday parties with my fabulous recipe.

You will need:
- ★ 225g milk chocolate
- ★ 175ml double cream
- ★ cocoa powder
- ★ a large mixing bowl
- ★ a wooden spoon
- ★ a small saucepan
- ★ a teaspoon

How to make:

1. Break up your chocolate and put it into a large mixing bowl.
2. Ask an adult to help you heat the double cream in a pan until it starts to boil, then ask them to pour it over your broken chocolate.
3. Ask your adult helper to stir until all the chocolate has melted.
4. Allow the mixture to cool in the fridge for four hours.
5. Once set, use your teaspoon to spoon out small amounts (big enough to pop into your mouth whole).
6. Roll the bitesize pieces in your cocoa powder until they are completely covered. If it gets too warm and difficult to roll, pop the mixture back in the fridge to set again.
7. Place all your finished truffles on a plate to set.
8. Enjoy straight away, or store them in the fridge for later.

You can also add drops of flavouring such as orange or peppermint, or even fruit such as raisins. Just drop these in before you allow the mixture to cool.

Chocolate cereal and raisin cakes

You will need:
* ✭ 60g unsalted butter
* ✭ 3 tablespoons golden syrup
* ✭ 100g milk chocolate
* ✭ 90g plain cereal (e.g. corn flakes, bran flakes, rice snaps)
* ✭ 50g raisins
* ✭ bun cases

1. Ask an adult to melt the chocolate in a bowl over a pan of simmering water, or in the microwave if you have one.
2. Ask your adult helper to add the butter in small pieces, and stir until melted, then remove from the heat.
3. Ask your adult helper to add the syrup and stir until mixed, add the raisins and stir until mixed, then add the cereal and stir very gently so they don't break up the pieces.
4. Spoon the mixture into your bun cases.
5. Leave to cool for 15 minutes, then enjoy!

(makes twelve cakes)

51

Become a fashion designer

I love fashion! I also love being creative, so I've started designing my own outfits. You can be a fashion designer, too. Just follow my advice and you'll have a famous fashion label in no time!

First, do some research. Get hold of as many magazines as you can and look at lots and lots of outfits. If you can, look online as well. What styles do you like? What kind of outfits are you drawn to?

Next, start a fashion scrapbook of all the outfits and accessories you like. Cut the outfits and accessories and stick them in, them out of magazines and stick them in, or print them from the internet. Younger Hello Kitty fans should always ask an adult for permission to use scissors, the internet and the printer.

ISSUE 3

YO!

cute★star
magazine

Once you have built up a scrapbook of clothes you like, you'll start to get an idea of your individual style: floral, classic, tomboy etc. Fashion design is all about creating your own individual style, so base your designs around the styles you like, and start sketching ideas for your very own outfits. It's best to start with a basic outline of the outfit first, then gradually add details. Once you get the hang of it you'll start to notice what works and what doesn't, and which details go together.

Hello Kitty Couture

Keep all your finished designs in one scrapbook. Choose a name for your fashion label and write it on the front of your scrapbook, e.g. 'Hello Kitty Couture'.

Now all you have to do is keep an eye out for fashion scouts! In the meantime you can always share your ideas with your friends.

Dress code dilemma

I need some help deciding what to wear this week. Can you help me choose which outfit to wear for each event? Draw lines between the events and the outfits to match them up.

Monday
Picnic

Tuesday
Family dinner

Wednesday
Rounders practice

Thursday	Friday	Saturday	Sunday
Fashion show	Sleepover	Thomas's fancy dress party	Cinema

Beauty sleep

A good night's sleep is a girl's secret weapon – it leaves you looking and feeling fresh. Here's how to make sure you get all the beauty sleep you need.

Remember to wash your face and brush your teeth before bed!

Read in bed for a while, until you feel your eyelids start to droop.

Don't have the heat up too high or down too low in your bedroom.

Have a glass of water by the bed in case you wake up thirsty.

Wear comfortable, loose-fitting pyjamas. Don't wear anything too tight as it will be uncomfortable and might wake you up.

Breakfast in bed

There's nothing better after a good night's sleep than a delicious and nutritious breakfast in bed. Here's how to make it for yourself, or as a treat for someone special:

You will need:
- ★ a tray
- ★ a tall glass
- ★ two bowls
- ★ a spoon
- ★ a small vase and one flower
- ★ muesli
- ★ milk
- ★ a jug
- ★ fruit salad (use small fruits or ask an adult to chop up fruit for you)

How to make:
1. Pour the muesli into a bowl.
2. Fill your jug with milk.
3. Add the fruit salad to your second bowl.
4. Fill your glass with orange juice.
5. Place everything on your tray.

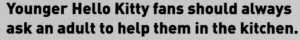
Younger Hello Kitty fans should always ask an adult to help them in the kitchen.

How well do you know Hello Kitty?

Think you know everything about me? Here's your chance to test your knowledge with this true or false quiz. For each statement, decide whether you think it's true or false, then tick the correct box.

1 Hello Kitty's star sign is Aquarius.

true   false

2 Hello Kitty lives in London.

true   false

3 Hello Kitty is as tall as five oranges.

true   false

4 Hello Kitty weighs as much as three apples.

true   false

5 Hello Kitty's twin sister is called Mimmy.

true   false

6 Hello Kitty lives with her grandparents.

true   false

7 Hello Kitty hates the colour pink.

true ✓ false ✓

8 Hello Kitty has been to Paris.

true ✓ false ✓

9 Hello Kitty has a brother called Thomas.

true ✓ false ✓

10 Hello Kitty's mother is called Mary White.

true ✓ false ✓

11 Hello Kitty's father is called James White.

true ✓ false ✓

12 Hello Kitty loves fashion.

true ✓ false ✓

Answers

I hope you enjoyed my 2012 Annual as much as I did, and that it's given you lots of ideas for the year ahead. Check below to see how you did on all the activities!

Page 12-13 Stage style

Page 20-21 Spot the difference

Page 22-23 Travel time

New York, USA

Kenya, Africa

New Delhi, India

Honolulu, Hawaii

Paris, France

Dublin, Ireland

Tokyo, Japan

Page 28-29
Simple Sudoku

Page 36-37
Messy Hello Kitty

Page 40-41
Apple maze

Page 34-35
What's in my handbag?

a. Mobile phone-10, **b.** Umbrella-7, **c.** Apple-1, **d.** Perfume-9, **e.** Spare bow-5, **f.** Keys-3, **g.** Purse-11, **h.** Notebook-2, **i.** MP3 player-6, **j.** Comb-8, **k.** Sunglasses-4

Page 58-59 How well do you know Hello Kitty?

1. False
2. True
3. False
4. True
5. True
6. False
7. False
8. True
9. False
10. True
11. False
12. True